APRIL
WIND
and
Other Poems

APRIL WIND

and
Other Poems

Frederick Turner

University Press of Virginia
Charlottesville and London

THE UNIVERSITY PRESS OF VIRGINIA
Copyright © 1991 by the Rector and Visitors
of the University of Virginia

First published 1991

Library of Congress Cataloging-in-Publication Data

Turner, Frederick, 1943–
April wind, and other poems / Frederick Turner.
p.   cm.
ISBN 0-8139-1358-6 (cloth)
I. Title.
PS3570.U69A85   1992
811'.54—dc20   92-21987
CIP

Printed in the United States of America

CONTENTS

Preface

This collection includes many of my shorter poems written in the eighties. It explores a connected group of ideas, feelings, and themes that are also the subject of the companion volume to this book, entitled *Beauty* (University Press of Virginia, 1991). There they appear in another modality as discursive essayistic prose. The two books are designed to shed light on each other, illustrating and explaining each other by a kind of neural and literary symbiosis. This symbiosis is itself discussed in *Beauty,* for instance in the sections on the ideographic and poetic-metrical neurocharms and in the general introduction to the neurophysiology of beauty in chapters 3 and 4.

The very form of these poems is directly indebted to the scholarly and scientific research into poetic meter that provided the starting point of the *Beauty* book. Most of the poems are composed in metrical form, ranging from the syllabics of "First Snow" and the dithyrambic-iambic irregular rhyme of "The Blessing" through the dactylic-trochaic pentameter of "The Blackness of the Grackle" to the strict iambic stanza forms of "Bone China Broken," "Untitled: To Mei Lin," and "On Goya's Saturn," and the various sonnets. In "The Cave at Zhoukoudian" a very elaborate scheme is followed, in which six six-line hexameter stanzas are followed by five five-line pentameter stanzas, four four-line tetrameter stanzas, three three-line trimeters, and then back to four, five, and finally six again to complete a chiastic, labyrinthine, concentric structure appropriate to its subject, the cave. In "Aphrodite" a sonnet emerges from free verse, like a butterfly out of a caterpillar; and in "First Base" the historical theme of the betrayal and redemption of classical values is echoed in a free-verse segment that cannot help breaking at one point into rhyme.

Thematically this book divides itself roughly into nine

sequences. The first treats poetically one of my most funda-
mental ideas about the nature of beauty: that our human
beauty-experience is the pleasurable recognition of a univer-
sal process of emergent orderliness that is also found in the
sciences of evolution and chaos theory. The second section
introduces what is both a corollary and an antithesis to the
first: the problem of the organic connection between evil,
conflict, and destruction on one hand, and beauty on the
other. The rest of the book examines ways of reconciling,
transcending, or accepting this contradiction.

The third section explores the idea of creative evolution,
as opposed to the static flux of the deconstructionists: it de-
fends poetically, as the *Beauty* book does philosophically, the
notion of teleology in nature. It also develops a poetic idea
of time in which our future descendants can in a mysterious
way serve retroactively as the guides of our spirit.

The fourth section is a celebration of the beauty of the
world as it is, a minute sensory observation of certain lovely
spots on our planet, together with a demonstration of how
meaning and value emerge out of sensory experience
itself—the body being part of the brain and the brain being
a neural maker of meaningful reality.

The fifth series of poems praises the central biocultural
relationship of our species, marriage and the family. The joy
of that relationship is directly related to the problematic and
even shameful juxtaposition of our animal and spiritual na-
tures. That juxtaposition is further explored in the sixth
group, whose central subject is the creative conflict between
sexual desire and spiritual love. Here, as in the prose book,
beauty and shame are shown to have a common root.

The seventh group takes up an implication in the pre-
vious group, which is the mystery and shame of personal
self-consciousness. Though the genre of these poems resem-
bles in some ways the "confessional" mode, their examination of the poet's self is not conducted for its own sake but
as a way of exploring experimentally the proposition that

beauty issues out of accepted shame. The boundary of the self is death: and the eighth group of poems finds both an epitome of and an escape from the problem of the self in the contemplation of death. *How* is death the mother of beauty?

The last group summarizes the whole passage through karmic attachment, sexuality, shame, and death to the mystical experience of beauty. This group concludes with two longer poems, in which historical and autobiographical contrasts between Europe and America become metaphors for the emergence of beauty out of conflict.

ACKNOWLEDGMENTS

Several poems in this collection first appeared in the periodicals listed below—whose editors the author wishes to thank.

Poetry: "On Gibb's Law," "Bone China Broken," "The Blessing," "The Distribution," "On Goya's Saturn." *Crosscurrents:* "The Blackness of the Grackle." *The Denver Quarterly:* "The Curse," "At the Front of the Jet," "Spirit Marriage," "Maine Summer, with Friends." *Yale Review:* "The Cave at Zhoukoudian." *Southern Review:* "April Wind," "On the Anthropic Principle," "37,000 Feet above the Atlantic," "Incarnateness." *Southwest Review:* "Aphrodite," "Early Warning." *Chronicles:* "Texas Rainbow," "For Mei Lin on Our Twenty-Second Anniversary." *Shenandoah:* "Freeze Tag," copyright 1984 by Washington and Lee University, reprinted from *Shenandoah:* The Washington and Lee University Review, with permission of the Editor. *Amazing Stories:* "The Expedition." *Gambit:* "English Renaissance Portraits." *New Hungarian Quarterly:* "On the Pains of Translating Miklós Radnóti." *Ontario Review:* "Glass—For Carol," "Pheromones."

I

On Gibbs' Law

If hot solution, saturate,
Be set upon a ledge to cool,
Rayed crystals will precipitate
On dust no thicker than a molecule;

When the slow chilling of the night
Crosses the threshold of the freeze,
The stars shine out as sharp and bright
As frostflowers in their fractal vortices;

The first white gas that was the world,
To ease the heat and press of birth,
Froze into forms as it unfurled:
The starry galaxies, the living earth;

Such pressure drives this crystal trance,
This thickening of art and hour,
Where order tumbles from the dance
Of dying syllables and forms a flower.

SELF-SIMILARITY

I listen to Bach's resonant concerto
For organ, oboe, strings, continuo,
As the car dives past stands of winter trees
Whose branches branch cascades of smaller V's.

The same disorder ordered into scales
Inheres within the cells, in the details
Of oaks and chinquapins, as in these naves
Of ribbed and vaulted sound, these mortised waves.

Flying by Greenland

In sheets and strands the pack ice spalls away
In a berg-fractal nether sky.
A dance of crazy mountains climbs the lands
Clapping their white hands.
Above, at the top of my window, glares
The snowfield, the exploding stairs
Into the daylight stars.
Cold on the window-plastic has embossed
A tiny archipelago of frost.

ORANGE LANTANA FIBONACCI REQUIEM

This morning the whole world is drenched with death.
Low fall hills burn to an orange powder,
Smudge the brilliant blueshroud of the sky.
And death is the rank gasoline it burns,
The musky, husky sour smell of leaving.
I break a sprig of lantana; it's got
Five orange brooches centered upon five
Jaune-yellow fivelobed masklets. They're deathmasks.
And the lantana smell's the inner scent
Of death's benzene ring, its sharp tomato-
Leaf, nightshade-and-basil, orange-skin ess-
Ence, its snaked cloisonné pentangle knot,
Its tail-eating snatch at perfection, its
Coming-around of the spirit, its gasp,
Its 3, 5, octane, its golden section,
Burning down to a white ash of diamonds.

II

THE BLACKNESS OF THE GRACKLE

The grackle is black as sin, he is like a religion,
he is Satany-satin, slick as the sail of a submarine,
he's a heat-sink, the anodized fin on the cylinder head.
The grackle collects the light, he collects information,
while about him the cosmos, slovenly, radiates energy.

The grackle recalls the black of earlier absences:
of the night, of the time when no eye recorded the lightfall,
of all other electromagnetic tones on the spectrum;
but he reaches back to bend those more primitive darknesses
to a greater sophistication: to state by not stating;

like the brilliant burn of the black of tropical fishes,
like the sable faces of certain macaques on display,
like the caves of the Ritual Primate, the funeral's raiment,
like subfusc, like Cary Grant's elegant easy tuxedos,
like the gold-crested lacquer scabbards of samurai swords.

The grackle's a black hole, the earpiercing wince of the
    anvil,
the pure click of an incompressible fluid imploding
and hitting itself as it meets in a clap at its center,
the creak and the splitting of timber, the crack of a timbre,
the berserker's shriek, the rip of heavy silk tearing,

in his strut, his effeminate deadly swagger, his waddle,
his enraged samurai waddle, his overdetermined,
his strenuous Hachiman entrance, the birdgod of warfare,
his lumbering takeoff, a jet fighter-bomber clearing
the runway under the maximum payload of armament;

and in all that blackness—matte-flocked as it would seem to
    be—

there seems only one thing that is radiant: his gold-milled
 eye,
like madness, hysteria, overcontrol, hyperthermia,
it's a concave disc to dissipate waste radiation,
the amberbright stare of a warning light showing at
 midnight;

till all of a sudden the whole point of the metaphor,
what his natural similes meant, is revealed in a flash,
as he spreads his wings and sinkingly measures his glide,
and his back blazes and flows in a wave of iridescence,
as a current discharges, leaving a blob in the eye:

his elegant dress, that requires no pigment to swagger,
but lets its grain fluoresce with waves of diffraction,
like a crowd drilled with cards to form the face of a leader,
like a blind, a burst of X-rays, a gold-trimmed bookedge,
reveals on the earth a sudden parcel of sky.

An Apology for the Poem
"The Blackness of the Grackle"

Friend, if my verses sometimes seem to praise
What is in nature savage as the fire,
A torment and a trial to our race,
A warning and reproach against desire;
If I have seemed too swiftly to rejoice
Not only in the lamb but in the pyre,
If I have given a finger and a voice
As gladly to the bow as to the lyre—
Forgive me, for I seek the hidden source,
That dreadful good called beauty, the frontier
From which all other goods and evils take their course;
Or else do not forgive me, though the tare
Is a seed as the wheat is; for the force
That generates them both is hard to bear.

THE CURSE

I was the Shah, Mohammad Reza Pahlavi.
I shall not speak of the place I now inhabit:
It is a vile thing to be carried and fed by those
Billion vulgar brains, to share their cells and dwellings,
Their memories so commonplace. The Peacock Throne,
The last siege of honor, is broken and thrown down.
And Allah, for why I do not know, hides His face
And I see Him not, the Merciful, though indeed
I never asked for mercy. That weak President
Was paying off a debt of shame, and he knew it.
I remember the gardens of Persepolis,
The roses and irises watered at great price,
Antique roses, gold pink as the ruins at evening:
Allah, perhaps, having given his Shahanshah
Command over paradises of the made world,
Denies to me the unmade and the eternal.
When I was a boy I turned my smooth cheek and chin
Stiffened by my little air force uniform
Against the baser uses of the world, and slew
My brothers, for they could not wield the skill of power
Nor bend the inner bow of necessary crime.
Before I made my Savak and sent it forth, I'd
Set upon my own flesh and spirit's malcontents
A crueler legion, more secret and much more pure:
An ichor of perfectest manhood that I paid
With icy carcinomas for; the dirty cells
That nourish life were crazed and thrown to confusion.
But all I did was for my loved kingdom, my Persia;
The middle land between Tabriz and Pakistan,
Between the Elburz and the Zagros, Gulf and Caspian,
My deserts and my whispering cedar forests,
My cities, Qom, Shiraz, and beautiful Teheran.
I swear it was not only the Sassanid pride,
Achaemenid obsession, but my love, that drove

Me to my land reforms, my women's equal rights,
My great purchases of American fighter aircraft.
I loved Iran as my two queens, wife and mother,
I loved her white arms, her terraces, her oases,
Her heavy date palms gilded by the April moon,
As much as Shah Jahan loved his Sheherezade.
I wept then, when my plane took off from Teheran.
But do not pity me, you billions, who retain the face
Of him who was once the anointed king of kings.
I leave you with the filthy Mullahs whose belief
Is tribute paid to terror of this fierce new world:
A tribute that I never paid. That storm they bring
Will blow down all your walls and bury them with sand.

BONE CHINA BROKEN

Suppose you're woken by a smash of glass:
The breaking of a china cabinet.
A bracket has fatigued beneath the mass
Of crystal, glazeware—coral, green and jet—
And overset
And tipped out this great chaos of regret.

The broken surface of fused kaolin
Beneath its glaze is porous, like fine bread.
We mock in forms foamy or crystalline
In manmade loaves and dishes, which are dead,
The spirited
And single shapes of life—leaf, fish, bird head.

If you should run a sliver of the glaze
Into your thumb, how copiously it bleeds.
Metabolism clots the injured place:
The jelly of our life is full of seeds.
Why must we needs
Prize thus our dead stones, metals, mirrors, beads?

Still, the glow falls from the emblooded skin:
Our bodies are more subtly frangible.
The soul's a mix, or an attunement, in
Plato's last portrait of his master's school:
A miracle,
A Fourier wave that passes, still stands still;

But when the lute is broke the chord is dumb.
You'll find your shattered china cuts the string
Of thought as sharply as it can the thumb;
Friends gave you that brown dish at your wedding:
It's now a thing
Cleft as their marriage was, that seemed so strong.

Or is it wrong to mourn the petty loss?
These plates are only leaves, and not the root;
Whole towns in flood, war, fire have borne the cross—
How do the poor folk cope, the destitute?—
Where, like Beirut,
The breakage is a kind of absolute?

For us, perhaps, the thing that we must bear
Is making gardens in a life that's level:
To love the painting on the jardiniere
—Antique dainty peonies—or the air-
White German china with the golden bevel,
The rice-grain celadon ceramic ware;
Even when evil
Meets with us there;
God's in the details; so is the noonday devil.

But is that mortal ache, uncleanliness
Of all possession, flesh or thing, the leaven
That quickens to a music life's duress?
Is hell, endured, in retrospect a heaven?
Does dung, even,
Perfect the glowing vessel in the oven?

This red pot was the last one left of three.
As soul imprints on flesh and flesh on things,
So those first two were kept in memory
When you would use the third. This breaking brings
Three shatterings;
And yet we seldom sell a dead man's things.

Do we wear out, our details once forgotten?
What neolithic heroine, her face
An immortal line not made but begotten,
Has left her dust to knit our potters' clays?

And are her days,
Her deeds, remembered any way with praise?

Is it enough her people left a sherd
Painted with wavy lines? and can that wave
Condense the spirit's savor in a surd?
Might a square inch of ivory then save
The precise curve
Of lovely human changing from the grave?

Sometimes we value china more than skin,
As heroes break their lives upon a word.
Flesh is more intricate than stone or bone,
And we are nothing if we're not absurd,
A china bird,
A tone struck from the crystal; half touched; heard.

III

Upon the Power of Certain Ideas

Now as the fulcrum holds, the forces come to bear,
The world obeys that rigorous conception
Which, having chosen out its sayer,
Shall bend the very axes of perception.

As in a martial art the body takes the print
Of some deep principle of torque and *chih,*
And in the stress of tournament
Exacts an excellence of purity,

Compelling both contender and antagonist
To trace the ancient pattern of a dance
Whose subtle leverage and twist
Wrung from the flesh of apes the human stance.

AGAINST APORIA

"There is no right way, no end of knowledge, no truth to be un-
veiled."
>—Marshall Brown: "Turning Points and the Dialectical
>Imagination," *Publications of the Modern Language Association of*
>*America,* January 1984

Nor can we reasonably say, Cratylus, that there is knowledge at
all, if everything is in a state of transition and there is nothing
abiding."
>—Socrates, in Plato's *Cratylus*

". . . man is creative only through love and in the shadow of love's
illusions, only through the unconditional belief in perfection and
righteousness."
>—Nietzsche, *The Use and Abuse of History*

Professors of aporia
And clerics of uncertainty,
You have brought forth the warrior
Who will reverse your history.

Truth, for you sedentary men,
Is altogether dangerous,
Committing you to where and when,
Demanding what is rigorous.

As if it were discovery,
Sages, you tell us all is change.
If all is change, how might there be
Anything we could call strange?

You are the always unsurprised,
The heroes of the Ph.D.:
Tissue that is never used
Turns quickly to malignancy.

And so your students, winged and fair,
Dew of the spirit on each limb,
Come to your studies of despair,
Depart shorn of their seraphim.

You spin your webs of apathy
There at the center of your maze:
But now the hero comes, and he
Will cut the knottings of your days.

Consider actors' innocence.
To play a part, they sacrifice
All their potentials to the dance,
Never the same performance twice.

Consider soldiers, who must give
Gallantly all experience,
That critics, safe at home, may live
To tax ten times what they did once;

Consider priests and athletes, who,
In mortal modesty and tact,
Still choose to be that which they do,
Refine the flesh into an act;

Take the chess master: should he touch
A piece not key to his attack,
He'll move it, and pretend that such
Was always the intended track;

The pilot of the *Challenger*
Falling in flames out of the sky,
Who knows, as California
Slides under, he must land or die;

The woman, laboring in spasm,
Senses there is no turning back,
Welcomes pain's nuptial orgasm,
Smiles twice as all her muscles crack.

An old man that I knew, when he
Felt that his death was come, the fool
Ran to its arms quite smilingly,
A diver sprinting for the pool.

Those dons and deconstructionists
Never close in, never commit;
Those actless revolutionists
Know only how to watch and sit;

Not children, for they cannot play,
Nor men and women, for they wait
And do not give themselves away:
As if, by that, they might cheat fate.

But Time will come and totalize
All the achievements of the breath;
Will spare the actors, bear the wise
To the aporia of death.

The Cave at Zhoukoudian

I.

Pekin Man

Flowstone, white calcite, gypsum needles, helictite:
The ancientest Pekin of jade and minarets.
We crawled in, stood. It's half a million years ago.
Shadows swept up like dark angels from our torches.
The stalactites had almost faces. Gods. Phalloi.
One saw glazed in stone the frown of an ancestor.

But when we left, after two hundred thousand years,
The place was full to the attic with our leavings:
Eighteen feet of ash; grass bedplaces; stone chips; bones.
Right at the bottom the great lantern jaws, femurs
Bowed out like whalebone, clumsy wrists and scapulars,
Skulls ridged like helms, cramped temporal cavities, spurs;

But in the upper levels there are fingerbones
Light in the knuckles, thighs straight for running, orbits
Finer for the glance of level eyes, jaw hinges
Made delicate by cookery, ample braincases.
And the tools: below, the hamhanded hammerstones,
Mallet-masses, a chip battered off for a blade;

Above, elegant leaf-flints, razorlike edges,
Awls, arrowheads, shavers faceted, polished, honed;
Evidence of design, percussion bulbs, culture,
The future modeled already in the white light
Of teleology, techne, art, that passion
That sets on the world a template, cuts off the rest.

And there he is in the ghost birdman of Lascaux,
And there she is, lovely, the head of Brassempouy;
Walls blazing with oxides, bone-black, manganese, iron,

Cupreous greens, red earths, Eve and Adam colors:
Ibex, bison, the dawn horse, wild cows galloping
And soaring over the moon; the rhinoceros.

Our ancestors. The Chinese call them "dragon bones,"
Use them for healing; not implausibly, for bones
Of Ramapithecus, crushed up and powdered, still
Can evoke antibodies in a living man;
Those lovers of rock crystal and vein quartz carried
Our gene sequences in their double helices.

II.

The Shadow Plays

The cave, for Plato, was an ignorance,
A place of darkness whence we must escape.
He was in love with perfectness and death
And in his geometric ecstasy
Forgot the glory of the human light.

Consider how the Javan shadow plays—
Radha and Krishna and the Pandavas—
Those pretty gilded puppets with long eyes—
Dance for the world a pattern lovelier,
Denser with time, than all geometry.

Amaterasu, lured forth from her cave
Only by greater caves of dance and mirror;
Airy Minoan mountain caves where Zeus
Hid Dionysus in the smell of bees,
Saffron, crocuses, poppy juice and fire:

These are the stories that we reconstruct
In builded grottoes frescoed with a dance,
Stupendous stupas, domes of blue and gold.

The stalagmites that twisted into dark
Became Bernini's bronze Baldacchino.

The Christ child in those frescoes lit a cave
Where we lay down as beasts and rose as gods;
Within the Altamiras of that dance
Polyphemos became Odysseus
And struck to fire the human heart and mind.

III.
The Mating Ritual

With drums of horn and flutes of straw
Matched with a clacking wooden bell,
They beat their feet upon the floor;
Their new, harsh voices rose and fell.

The strange rites of baboons and birds
Might rank the tribe and mark the bond;
Our ancestors were drunk on words:
Their genes bent to the dark beyond.

The brutish ones could not behave,
Nor chant the rubatos of the night;
Cast out from the tribal cave,
Their seed died in the stupid light.

Like refined breeds of dog or fowl,
We strained ourselves into our fate:
The beast whose genes are cultural,
We learned this when it was too late.

IV.
The Birth of Time

A photon is a drone:
Scarcely a thing of time.
The leptons hum one tone.

Crystals are more sublime:
Their harmonies of stone
Preserve them like a rhyme.

But humankind alone
Spans in its song all time,
Survives the death of bone.

V.
The Gentle Fetish

KALOS is the myelin
Quickens the fibers of our race;
Value's not got by laboring
But seen like beauty in a face;

Our species makes a web of worth
Out of the threads of fantasy;
Obediently our pliant earth
Vests in the new economy.

The puritan, postmodernist,
Is not the enemy of flesh:
Rather, he hates the fetishist
Whose dancing spins the human mesh.

The loveliness of cheek and breast,
Of eye and lip, were bought by death

That risks the good to get the best
And passes on the choicest breath.

VI.

The Eyetalian Caves

I heard this story once while hitchhiking.
The scene's important: on the Interstate
That runs along the valley of the Platte.
The land's so flat there's nothing but barbed wire,
They say, between your jacket and the Pole.

"What's that?" I asked, pointing to some low bluffs.
"That's the Eyetalian Caves," the driver said.
It seems an immigrant from Tuscany
Had settled with his wife and children here
To get a living as a shoemaker.

In the first year the polar winds came down
And carried off his children and his wife.
He got a little strange and never spoke.
Later he bought the land around the bluffs
And started digging labyrinths of caves.

No one knew why. He roofed them all with brick,
And dumped the tailings under the huge sky.
After some years the cobbler died. The curious
Found nothing in the caves but caves.
Young men would take their girls there for a while;

Then for a time the place lay visitless.
When somebody last looked, the rattlesnakes
Had made the place a breeding ground, and coiled
In their thousands in the Eyetalian Caves.
Perhaps, I thought, this artist wanted home.

VII.
The Measure

Events are real in physics if they're measurable.
All objects measure other objects and themselves
According as their sensitivities allow.
To go on measuring is, as such, to survive.
The contents of the present are what has endured.
The great survivors are the knowers of themselves.

And the determiners of that which is are those
That feel and know their world within them most of all.
They are the future-makers, for it's they who call
The indeterminate to place and force of being.
From light and energy through matter, life and mind
The knowers of themselves evolved and grew;

But kept a record of their path inside themselves
Set in the ordered hierarchy of organism.
Thus crystals, template-beings, reproduce themselves
And the life-helix peels, prints off its pattern, takes
To its own self an outward shape that shapes the world:
This densest shapeliness of being is beautiful.

Sweetest of all, the moment when the rules which hold
Each level of the hierarchy within its place—
Of syntax, composition, tempo, meter, form—
Seem to be broken, and the match between one and
The other will not hold, but rising from the interference
Is a new, ghostly form made out of moiré waves.

Within the cavern of the skull the world takes shape;
Within the caves and temples of community
The many other worlds of might and ought and shall
Painted or sung or danced, even hypothesized,
Grow, reproduce, risk their rebirth in sex and death,
Fed by the drunken honeys of the brain's rewards.

So beauty, then, is truth?—the highest measurement,
Survival in its own most comprehensive sense.
It was no freakishness that formed the human brain,
That organ tuned to beauty as the eye to light,
To make and feel the hierarchy of time, and most
To look upon and love another human face.

37,000 FEET ABOVE THE ATLANTIC

Here between heaven and heaven there is no prayer,
No mark of past, no roots, as those I saw
Just yesterday, great feet mottled and bare
Thrust in the sandy soil of Hanover:
Only the breath of ego and the smell
Of coffee, and the sound of broken air
Tearing across the airfoils and the hell
Of carbide turbine-blades. And yet I swear
The darkened heavens whisper to me here
Of you, rapt in your blue pavilions,
Bone-temples deep with your divine software,
And what you will have known, what alien suns,
What techne of what gentleness and power;
And the stunned self, its great gifts stranded here
Between the nightblue future and the past,
Is silent in the vision of the knower
Where the first heaven is whispered by the last.

On the Anthropic Principle

If all was as it was at the beginning
Because its consequence must be its cause,
Being is but the foreghost of becoming,
Freedom the future source of present laws.

And if our ancestors must ratify
Their being by begetting memories,
They sing themselves to being as they die
And we fulfill their ancient prophecies.

And if this moment is the spring of what
Will one day call our moments into being,
They walk among us, potent, lovely, not
Yet born, and shape our seasons with their seeing.

THE NEW AGE

They say there is a new age coming,
They say that peace is now at hand;
They say the wheels of time are humming
And form harmonic patterns on the land.

And the Press howls at them, and crowns them
With paper carnival and crepe,
And surely they are right to hound them,
Being such babies in the ways of hope.

But if reality might answer,
If that long road might be cut short,
If the unborn we call the Dancer
Should out of pity leave his shining court,

Our child the Son of Man in splendor
Reach back into this ancient time
And touch the brutes that did engender
Him, with music quickening the slime;

Then would it not be something churlish
If observance were not done?
Were not that other virgin foolish
When all the lamps are shining as the sun?

THE ARCHAEOLOGIST

This summer he's an archaeologist.
The planet shimmers with an alien star,
The star of Texas, fire in its fist:
Huge lies, here, are the only truths there are.
The doors whoosh shut when he goes in and out.
His shirt cuffs start at once to curl and char
(Texans too proud to wear a pressure suit
When moving from the airlock to the car).

The light is more than mortal eyes can know.
The bare caleche glitters like the moon.
The salamander-men from Mexico
Sing mariachi in the blaze of noon
And plant the salamander-trees and raise
A thousand homesteads every afternoon.
You see two hundred miles through the haze;
The sky bellows like a rubbed balloon.

This Dallas house is like an icy tent,
A place of whitened shade and turning fans.
The archaeologist, its resident,
Retires here to formulate his plans.
Within, it's silent, ceiling-lit, and cool.
Only the hum of great machines reminds
The dweller of the daily miracle
Of science and the work of human hands.

Each night he dreams the house might blow away;
The desert wind that sears this latitude
Has in his dreams burnt it to silver-grey,
Rolled it across the plain, a tumbleweed:
No human being ever slept before
Here in this flat sun-shot infinitude;

Even the night is like an open door
Where fields of barren galaxies recede.

This summer he's an archaeologist,
But what he excavates is air and time.
He is no digger in the stony past,
But one whose work it is to scour the grime
Of present centuries from future things,
And show how graceful boulevards will climb
Across this prairie on their glassy wings,
Blown by a forest-breath of beech and lime.

Sometimes the future air will crystallize
Upon him, where a pyramid of glass,
An arch of leaf-thin granite, will arise
Out of the seething present, and confuse
The careful measurements of year and will.
At evening, like a laser, light will pass
From the sun's ruby through the dazzling grille
Of a facade, a trouble to his gaze.

And he has found already signs and wonders.
He's pieced together fragments of a God
Which show diffraction-traces of His Thunders
And electronic circuits from His Rod.
The human species then will choose, it seems
To be for some millennia quite mad
And make itself an Allah of its dreams,
Until it wearies of it, like a fad.

And he has found sweet polytheisms,
Golden-thighed princes of the Texan seas,
Saints of the future, painted animisms,
Apotheoses into beasts and trees;
He's reconstructed their symposium
And trapped a suite of possibilities,

Cultured them in a secret medium
And set them dancing in a graceful frieze.

And there's a hoard of horned, gigantic bones,
Falstaffian and Pantagrueline,
Together with a buckle made of bronze,
A turquoise tieclasp and a diamond pin
Belonging to the fabled Texas Liar
Who brings to being all there has not been,
The booster with the billion-dollar lyre,
The poet of the not yet genuine.

Sometimes the archaeologist is lost
In those blue parklands, those suburban climes
Where in their evening dress, at Pentecost,
The merry knights await what sign the times
Will bring to them, what wonder or what quest.
He stumbles then among them with his rhymes,
His airy shovel, and his second-best,
And begs to be forgiven for our crimes.

IV

EARLY WARNING

Spring comes in Dallas like a gunshot, like
A big transformer fuse, a missile strike.
Ninety degrees. Over the northern grid
Dances a disembodied pyramid.
Foam and dark water dries up in a flash
On the white-hot forecourt of the car wash.
Air has the lilac tremor of cocaine,
Matter's dissolved to flakes of cellophane.
All along Hillcrest and Arapaho
Rises, pinkwhite, a radioactive glow
Of blanched pearblossom, apple, plum and quince,
Black redbud cankered with flushed innocence.
Don't drive there with the window open; you'll
Fall sick with the flower fumes. It's April Fool,
It's mayday, mayday. Photochemical,
The Carolina jasmine's cadmium fireball
Batters the sidewalk with a yellow shock
Releasing a sweet gas of poppycock.
The crocuses poke up their noses. "Urk!"
They gasp, and open with a purple jerk.
Don't know if that's blue sky or a fresh storm
The sun shines into, giddy, white and warm.
Yes, it's a cloud. The weather map has grown
A newborn thunderworld all of its own,
Mushrooming up, neon and shadowhazy.
Out of it hail will tumble soon like crazy.
It smells of black disk-brake powder, of guns,
Of pyramids and glass and pentagons.
Better take shelter in an underpass.
City of all desires, city of glass.

AT THE FRONT OF THE JET

The grapefruit's fresh, the coffee's coarsely ground,
The lunch comes with a cold aperitif;
The cushioned takeoff scarcely makes a sound
More vexing than the "iff" that ends "Braniff."

Up front the stewardesses really care.
They have kind eyes, like guides in Disneyland.
(Doctors, great statesmen, writers go by air:
The people at United lend a hand.)

And at the terminal a car is waiting,
Blue windshield showing a fresh trace of suds;
They've left the blower on, refrigerating;
The tape deck breathes "Moon River"; the door thuds.

Give me the sole, the prime, the demitasse.
Yes; if God travels, then He goes first class.

THE HYDRANGEAS AT STRESA
—for Amy Clampitt

Enchant, lacustrine littoral,
Latin Verbano, veiled Maggiora;
Mist-terraces magnolial, ·
Enchant, dewed, aromescent flora;
From this Piedmontane hither shore
Let drenched and drawn-up memory
Look as it lingered once before
Across the gloam to Lombardy;
Let, as crepusculate the lake
Engulfs the vapors of the squall,
The Borromean islands take
Their naviformae cameral;
Let that white solar-radiate plate
Of snow on the etheric sheer
Glimmer again within the slate
Goose-rippled water of the mere;
Lend to the nostril's exigence
The coffee bushes' tarragon,
Those clustered lemons' flower scents,
Hanging cedars of Lebanon;
Let tulip trees lift up their cups
About Pompeian red facades,
Where cupreous or prussic drops
Fall in hydrangean cascades;
And give to memory that seed
Rubious and pomegranate,
Which, broken, makes the summer bleed
Once more its sweet ejaculate.

ON ISOLA MADRE

Inland quiet. Talk over the rise.
The vaporetto's silenced by the point:
It won't be back till four.
Upon their blue and bluer skies
Lean the Italian Alps. A huge door
Of seaside air has shut out all the sound,
As if the altitude had bound
The eardrum with its rarity, and made it faint;
The lake, a little wall of sky blue paint,
Locks in the garden ground.

No Poem on Greece

When Greece was but a fiction, I could sing:
The lime and rosemary of Arcady,
The green and liquid light that swam within the sea,
The smoky taste of everything;

Then the gods' faces turned and smiled at me,
Their sightless eyes stared through the veil of being:
For absence from the known had been the price of
      knowing,
Two obols that the eyes might see.

But now the light of Greece has blinded me,
The taste of Greece has quite bound up my tongue,
Its smell has burned the pharynx and the roots of song
With a hot alchemy;

For such a difference there is, between to see
And be.

LAST EVENING IN CALIFORNIA

My planet lies before me here so innocently.
She's twisted down her wavelengths on the evening
until the skyline is a powdery crimson.
The conifers lay out precise black lace.
O planet, why did you trim your hills
with downy mists? Why does a star
stand at the zenith brilliant where, forty words before,
was only an electric blue?
Your sleepy pigment's thickened, and the color
saturates certain cells and throws the radiant acres
into a single ray of green. An air creeps past
smelling of nothing, till the aftertaste
of it sharpens to miles of pungent straw
that have baked to golden in a welled velour.
Planet, matched to me so magically,
time and again I put you on like raiment,
taking your satins and your silks upon my skin;
but then impatient with my time, I cast you off,
sweet living spirit, passing from land to land.
But you play me the bed trick every time,
most faithful wife, slip into the guise
of the rose witch Circe, the nymph Calypso,
so when I make my journeys, every landfall's home
and every lover's passionate Penelope.
These honey skylights, golden hills,
these touches of the air are your dear body
that I can never leave.

AMARYLLIS
—for Tom and Mark

Out of the gnarled foot,
out of the fleur-de-lis of tongues,
there shoots a fork of jade flesh,
two ovoid pylons, each braced with a shin.
One soars to a green wrist, swells to a long glans
whose head's a right whale's lips, a toucan's bill.
The other has broke open and let free
a furled bullet, candy-striped with pink,
and a huge vulva, a double trinity,
six shells of glittering crepe,
whose vertices are ribbed with emerald,
whose throat's as rosy as a conch.
Out of its tonsil thrusts a clump
of stalked phalloi, each tipped with a pollened wad.
The amaryllis, though, secretes no drop of perfume;
only about it you will find the air is delicate.

MAKESHIFT SPRING

Whoever sketched this springscape was in a hurry.
The drop scene's burlap and ply is scarcely dry:
a mist of the wrong green put on with a spray,
smudge of dirty white—a flowering cherry—
debris everywhere, chalked twigs, wet branch highlights,
a sky all the shades of the palette have got mixed;
and a very beautiful actress with expensive perfume
and a cigarette has just wandered through the set.

Spring Evening

Above the baby powder clouds
The sky is china blue.
Soon, young and chattering, the crowds
Of stars come pushing through.

And this is the first dispensation,
The setting up of the odds;
This is the eve of creation,
This is the time of the gods.

Texas Rainbow

Solemn, unbent, an arch of rays,
A rigid shaft of curvature
So perfect, yet so dim upon the air,
Has purified the haze

And given all its pointed light,
Its wink and tinctured shimmerings,
To edge and sharpen out these earthly things
In a sneeze of delight.

Our life's a mother-liquid, and
Its solute and its golden leaven
Falls from the fading sacrifice of heaven
Over the greenbright land.

V

DANIEL AND CLAIRE GO RIDING IN THE PRAIRIE

Where did it come from, this pale skin,
This tall quixotic gallant strain
Among my moody Chinese kin,
This that I mixed my seed with, and my grain?

I see them riding side by side,
My son with his long back and hand,
My niece, white-freckled, dignified,
With the same fine desperate self-command.

All beauties now seem faint beside
Those essences of personhood
That float apart or coincide
According to the genes' vicissitude.

Their silence and their sudden smile,
Their brown eyes and their length of bone,
Their calmness with the animal,
Their singleness, as one who walks alone,

Denote the *puer* still intact,
Puella candid as the flower,
That through the mixing and the act
Preserve the soul's perfection and its power.

MAINE SUMMER, WITH FRIENDS

A wind as white and clear as glass
Shakes and shivers the windowpanes.
The woman on her honeymoon
Leans to pull shut the frame;
It captures a green aspen branch
And the room's full of quaking leaves.
Her husband's traveling in the west—
We joke about this at breakfast.
Our hosts have been briefly parted.
I must phone my wife long distance.

The strange sea crawls between headlands
Blue as a dream. The cellar here
Is half full of a granite hump.
Hard to tell if you're warm or chilled,
Like in a long sweet marriage, if
The grief is a spat, or boredom,
Or the pain of excessive love,
Warm wind of spring or cold summer.
And we are so close to the sound,
To the charged, lifetaking sea.

And the children, the house is full,
Often, with sleeping children: fate
In its softest guise, the signed mark
Of generation; embarrassing
To us fools who came together
Driven to that work by more than
Breakfast table conversation.
Nevertheless, on this margin
Between the dark woods and the sea
We try to come to know our friends.

DRY NIGHTS

That was the last poor rag of babyhood:
The way his bed stank like a fox's set;
That easy flow of innocence he could
Let fall from him while all his body slept.
We do him wrong to colonize his dreams!
Can we afford to lose that alienness,
Those strange, limestone-bright coasts, lands without
    names,
And brush away his wilds with a caress?
Lately he sat up in the barber's chair
Swathed like a businessman, and smiled with such
Clownish lopsidedness that I laughed there
In the saloon to see this Stan Laurel, much
Reduced, his face wide open, his cropped hair;
And afterwards could scarce forbear to touch.

To Ariadne

I am your elder lover.
I know not what to say.
What image could recover
your manner and your way?
For what is like you, who
are colored like all things,
Taking their colors to
the dark quilt of your wings?
Should I describe your speech,
whose thousandth part might be
Fractioned again, and each
more branched than any tree?
When nothing that you are
speaks openly or free,
How may so dark a star
be gauged by one like me?
My elder mistress, you
resemble but one kind:
The winding of the clue,
the labyrinth of mind.

UNTITLED: TO MEI LIN

How should I move my mouth who am compelled
To speak of that whereof one cannot speak?
In dreams we have beheld
Entities, shapes without a name—
Not those vague dreams, whose images are weak
As water on a glass, but those that claim
The passions of great love or shame,
And yet we know not how their hues and tastes are
    spelled—
Just such a thing is this that I have held.

I've woken with such words upon my tongue
As *shathe, encission, arcuate, mascale,*
And as when I was young
I'd play with words, or as the poet, mark
Some lovely Magyar word—*virág, halál,*
Csavargo, ringatózom, hallgatok—
I felt the light of sense go dark
Just as I groped for the last shreds of it that clung
To a strange music that might yet be sung.

What is a thought, before the branching ways,
Whose track and being it is, have taken shape?
A path, before the blaze
That makes it one? a gift or skill
Sleeping within the germ cells of an ape,
That, with a future violin, or quill,
Or aerofoil, or compass, will
Capture the palm, the oak, the myrtle or the bays?
What is a seed before the game it plays?

How shall I say, my mistress, what you are?
Look at the low sky when a deck of cloud
Is lit to cinnabar

By city lights, sodium red:
See how that strange rift in it has allowed
(A princess in a country of the dead)
Space for the white moon in its bed
Of sweetest blue, and how these darkened wonders are
Caught in a rainpool with the evening star.

When I was growing up in Africa,
Lemon and melon jam was all my joy.
Around the opener
The mild green syrup oozed, and bled
On the sour edge and label. What the boy
Could taste, I tasted; but the taste has fled.
Now from that country of the dead,
Brought back and altered to your voice and character,
The warm green cubes remember Africa.

The fruit smell of a sawn-off Christmas tree.
The flavor of a guava, cold and suave.
A simple melody
That I shall hear upon a train
Next year, sung in a language stressed like Slav.
What does an angel smell of? Of the rain?
Think how the pumping burn of pain
Melts with the shock of morphine to the brain, and see
How you perform your alchemy on me.

Compare us with all other animals, and we
Are old, ancient beyond imagining;
We're terrifyingly
Intentional, mysterious,
Swift as the shrew's thin whisker, glittering,
As sensual as is a succubus,
In calculation devious,
Capable of caresses that subdue the free
With their addictive purpose and decree.

And being thus, is it a wonder still
That you should, in your limbec or your mesh,
Concentrate and distill
Dream essences that have no names,
Meanings whose words have never taken flesh?
Those younger lovers cannot know the games
That we, the servants of the flames,
Play on the self-consuming instruments of will,
Where an old moon rides in the darkening chill.

The Blessing

Sometimes sweet life presses too closely on the soul.
Sometimes love's muscles ache
With a familiar paralysis,
And any effort makes us spasm and shake:
The milky acids, that control
The mechanism of exhaustion, burn
For their purgation in forgetfulness.
Like little poems that fatigue
The spirit, folding it too often upon one turn,
The small twistings of happiness
Bend us close to our break.
I've taken artist's vows that I'd not speak
About the mere coincidences of my life:
Reader, you're not a priest; I'll not confess
What I'd not mention to my wife.
The anecdote of personal existence dies
—Should die, unless
The senses' genius pranks it in some freak
Of unrecordable loveliness
That reaches outward to eternity;
Or if philosophy
Or if the flame of God consumes
It utterly;
Or if the wise heads of my sons
Conceived in those intelligent and graceful arms
Take it and make it more than me.
That night the moon's
Light blew in the southern wind
Under an airy roof of clouds. I'd see,
As eyes grew bright as mind,
The names engraved upon the stones,
The distant lamplight caught within a face
Of polished granite in the burying ground.
Romantic place!

I'd come there vaguely to escape the pain
Of mortal happiness.
But in that village of the dead,
Farmers and loving wives, insurance men,
I did not feel afraid:
What could they do to me?
And suddenly
My eyes lifted to the naked woods around:
It was a carnival of family fires,
The many homes of colleagues, neighbors, friends:
Hillsides of dining tables, telephone wires,
Lit porches, darkened garden plots, and bowls of flowers.
Here where I stood outside it all, a ghost, beyond the ends
Of the earth, I turned and loved it once again.
That strange kitchen, the red
Counter with the lamp, the tall chairs,
The lady with the book, I knew as mine.
I had no mortal cares;
My body, calm as air, became a sign.

ON GOYA'S SATURN

—for Edwin Watkins

That god who stares from the picture space
As if he—only now it's done,
The madness slaked—can recognize the face,
Whose blood and brains he gulped, to be his son,
Catches the humanist's eye.

Chronus, blind time, knowing himself again
To be Kronos the wretched king,
Squirms like a frog across the void. His pain
Goya suggests in the stiff dance he's doing;
The darker shape of why

Is shadowed in the history of Spain.
The deed of sacrifice once done
Is such as never can be done again.
The naked body of the beloved son
In his sire's hand must die.

And many kingdoms of the past have died
Choked by the monuments they raised:
Eternity bought by infanticide,
An immortality of being praised.
The fierce Spanish sky

Towers like fate over exhausted fields;
The gold they wrestled from the sun
Wasted the factories and burnt the guilds.
All that the dark conquistadors had won
Time swiftly would deny.

The traveler, though, is not content at last.
There is an immortality

That looks, not to the future, but the past.
His own exacted, but willed, piety
Gives history the lie.

We can be deathless backwards, then, says he.
And now he shivers, for he knows
Across the waste of every century
The high and fiery fellowship of those
Carved in lapis lazuli.

There are three kinds of immortality.
Electromagnetism's one:
It neither lives nor dies. The family tree
Makes two: my seed's my father and my son.
The last is memory.

He calls to mind a fable he once read:
There's been a thermonuclear war,
And Greece, by good luck, among all the dead,
Had not been scathed. Two scholars hear the roar
From the grove at Delphi.

After the grief, the known loss of sons, wives—
Scorched basements, as they come to know,
All that is left of their American lives,
New-vacant wavelengths on the radio—
They find that they must die

Only more slowly than the world they mourn.
Although the heaven is blue, and Greece
Seems to lie glowing in the sea newborn,
The sickness that's too pure to call disease
Beams from the perfect sky.

And so they haste in their last weeks to see
Parnassos and Mount Helicon,

The pleasant vales of pastoral Thessaly,
And, last, Olympus, shining in the sun.
They now begin to die.

But through that perfect summer, goatsmilk cheese
And souvlaki and Samian wine
And olives, resin—all the grace of Greece—
In dialectic's helical design
They slowly learn to fly:

The riddle is that Oedipus's quest
Leads to the breaking of the atom;
The analytic wisdom of the West
Stems from one trivial desideratum:
Asking the question, Why?

And in the company of Socrates,
More and more plainly real and strange,
They learn to little reck the world's decease.
The ideal forms survive the death of change.
They are in ecstasy.

At last—the story goes—no marrying
Now, nor giving in marriage, so
We see the stronger comrade carrying
His friend, embracing him, as lovers do; the glow
Of a Greek evening sky.

The traveler remains unsatisfied.
The fable in his memory
Cannot shake off its loneliness and pride.
Men make a kind of immortality
Without a woman by;

But like boy-soldiers who know how to die
And have not learnt a way to live

With their slight sacrifice they'll dignify
A vulgar ideology with what they give.
The traveler is I.

All of a sudden I am forty-five.
The layered myth of babyhood
Is further than the last hours I shall live.
The absence of myself, not understood
Till now, comes with a sigh.

I must escape. How? Clothe myself with laws
Till their stiff raiment, of its own,
Stands when the flesh is spent? and lock the doors
Of change, a holy figure carved in stone?
That was Kant's lullaby.

Or plunge into the Heraclitan fire
Joining the changelessness of change?
Or in the tragic mask, upon a pyre
Take to myself my fate? Is it not strange
How the I clings to I?

I know a man, the wisest of his time,
Who when I asked him which he'd choose
Between loved persons and a deathless rhyme,
Answered "the poem." To leave a name, he'd lose
Wife, children, family.

And that's his weakness, though I honor him.
The little lacking of the man
Like the untimely withering of a limb
Pays for the flight of the Olympian.
It's a great gift, to die.

All we can do is pour the spirit on the ground.
The traveler, the humanist,

Has held his sick baby in his arms, and found
The mystery that metaphysics missed:
No heaven in the sky

But the sheer toil of living as a wife,
Banal repeated sacrifice,
The long humiliation of a life
Known intimately by another's eyes,
The fruitless hushabye;

The need to judge, when all is relative,
And not to need too much, unless
Your lover, heartsick, has a need to give—
But then the shining in the baby's face,
And dawning in his eye.

The world's life does not grow along a line.
The future of the settled past
Dies with the past itself. We redefine
By love the very laws of time, recast
The pattern of the sky.

The sages, we, and those who left no name
Share in the human Word divine.
And burning in the freshness of the flame
Like water turned by toil and love to wine,
We learn at last to die.

FOR MEI LIN ON OUR TWENTY-SECOND WEDDING ANNIVERSARY

When you were twenty-two a messenger,
Who said a king had sent him, came to you,
Set in your hands a book before you were
Ready to answer him, what you would do;

And said the book was strange as it was rare,
And she that opened it must first be sure
Of her heart, to live what was written there,
Or else the king would die that very hour;

And that the book must faithfully each day
Be tended with pure water and with light,
Its chamber swept with brooms lest it decay,
Its virtue vanish in the shades of night.

Twenty-two years, my love, not knowing if
The messenger told truth or told a lie,
You kept the book in honor, as a wife
Might keep a husband; lest the king should die,

You never opened up a single page,
Uncertain of your heart, if it were true;
Patient beyond your youth, beyond your age,
You will yet wait another twenty-two.

VI

April Wind
—for Ann Weary

Wind, gigantic, wrestles the April leaves;
The mares are nervous, elated, tossing their manes;
We pass in file under the forest eaves
Where a magic bodarc shakes an emerald free
From each of its branched black veins;

The path is narrow, we are fingered at elbow and knee
By the grape and the cedar elm. All goes dazzling bright:
The sun has come out and now we suddenly see
How this green is the white of the plant world, the blanch
Of its secret kinship with light;

And my friend turns—the artist, who owns this ranch—
And tells how a painter will throw on a gout of white,
And feather a green glaze thereover, for a branch;
And now, strangely, we both fall silent and ride
As if we were chilled by a slight;

For through the woodland is blowing a perfume, a tide
Of sweetness from some blossoming out of our sight,
Mysterious, innocent, heavenly, known on the inside
Only, unfading; and the mares are dancing, and we,
Like disciplined riders, pull tight

On the rein and grasp with the strength of the thigh and the
     knee
The huge bodies that move, prehistoric and blind,
Through the now darkening glades. And we are quite free
To speak, or not, as we make for the gate we shall find
In the waves of the fragrant wind.

SPIRIT MARRIAGE

—for Lynda

Those dancing little feet are not
The dancing feet of my bride.
They are the dance of one who caught
The world's gods in her side.

That skin of ivory and cream is not
Her skin between my sheets.
It's the integument of thought,
The bridal-cloth of supernatural sweets.

The eyes, so shocking, black, and hot,
Are Brahman-visitors, the gnostic Yes,
The speculative lamps of heaven, but not
Wet to the eyelashes with my caress.

And that giddy gasp, that laugh, is not
The catch of passion's breath; nor
Is the sigh, the expiration, what
An earthly lover lingers for:

They are the signs of one who sought
A truth, or a lovely line of verse,
And found them when they were forgot
And made them hers.

That paradise we shared was not
The heaven of the sharers of the flesh:
It was the innocent garden-plot
Of poetry, so dawning and so fresh.

The golden tree we plucked was not
The veined trunk of the body's serpentry:

It was the friendship-bought,
The simple, apple tree.

The bright and dark-eyed children we begot
Are not the fruit of kind or of desire:
They are the seraph-knot
Of the holy fire.

GLASS
—for Carol

I learn that glass can be compared to the soul.

Glass is the slowest liquid, and will pool
and swell across its lowermost diameter;
yet more elastic than is rubber or fine steel,
and yet, again, brittle and liable to flaw.

A steel wheel scarcely grazes it, for steel
is softer than the glass; the pressure makes a wake
within the dilatory fluid, and the molecules
shift and make way invisibly, and one may take
the graven sheet between the thumbs, and lightly press
and draw apart, and snap it soft as candy;
and there are now not one but two pieces in your hands.

Glass imitates the crystal's high immutability,
yet cracks, not along predetermined planes as crystals do,
but unpredictably according as electrons share their fields;
and quite unlike a crystal, howsoever slow, it flows.

The pigment though, in glass, is perfecter
and faster, fused and laminated in by fire,
than any surface coloring; the artist loves
the colors of the glass, for they are clean,
and you can see the very light itself by which it glows.
And thus the artist takes the Sun itself, the little god
of this our local shrine of light within the galaxy,
and makes a workman of it, or a medium.

Yet glass deceives the eye, by seeming absent
when it stands obstructing other energies
than light, as common matters do. Artist of light,
of glass, please do not graze me, even lightly,
lest I break; yet you have shown me that I flow.

The Lover of Women
—for Jan

After all the wisdom, all the purification,
the thought and the discipline, the long burning to perfume
of everything fleshly, the mommacells rising like scales of
lard, yet chastened and shrunk by the rod of the spirit,
still I find I'm in love with every woman.
We, the male, are the half-apelike sex;
with our sprouting tuftwads of hair, our deep musculature,
the red lights of aggression and lust, the ache of
perpetual unsatisfied rage and display, our kindness
born of the long struggle for mastery over our
impulses—we, the male, still yearn for the godfolk,
the ancient childrenlike ones, the smooth-skinned, the
    subtle,
beautiful, self-absorbed ones, who understand all human
    motives,
who have long served us undeserving, as Adam was served
by the angels; the long-lived ones, their eyes brilliant with
knowledge, their bodies softer and smaller like nobles,
like princes, the divine children, whose tutors have taught
    them
languages, delicate crafts, dominion over the
great truths of beauty, of death, of passing
on over into children; and I love them, I love them all,
the old and the young, their passion, their bravery; how
    they see
in the world its moments of sweetness, its strangeness, its
    darkened
gathering in, when we look at the strangers in cars and
love them, each for his oddity, each for his piece of the
madness of heaven; how they make around them rituals,
Christmas nights, the smile of the rose virgin of
Chartres; and how lovely they are, with their breastlets,

their long, vulnerable waists, their fresh and open
faces, like divine infants, grave with the human
knowledge; how they're so swift to embrace, to give, in
    spite
of themselves, how worldly they are, how hopelessly
    realistic.
And all I would wish, given the unhoped-for offer
of heaven, would be to sit on a coign and hear their voices
and smell the angel smell of their bodies (not always
so sweet after all) and watch them move, the god–children,
their fingers touching, touching the rims of the flowers.
And if this lover of women should be banished for such
    desires,
censured from heaven because of his disrespect, the
annoying power of his gaze (though quite unintended),
nevertheless he would think of them always happily,
    happily
there in whatever corner of hell he's condemned.

PHEROMONES

A perfume on the running track
Breathed, stranger, from a secret place,
Passes across to this old jock,
Makes him a moment to break pace.

Is it the white crease underneath
The bosom in its lightsome tent?
The delicate and curly wreath
Dewed in its warm environment?

What strawberries, mademoiselle,
What arum lilies do you grow?
How does your little garden smell
So sweet, so celibate, and so

Of other species than the male?
What essence then do you distill,
That makes your flesh so fine and pale,
And strangely stamps your alien will?

And as I pass, your brave small smile
Carries a faint trace of a fear:
I am a brute so to beguile
This lady as I have done here,

To know along the scent she wears
The alien ichor of her sex:
Madam, dismiss your anxious cares,
And let me offer my respects.

Or do you, running, catch a breeze
Of that dark liquor of the male?
Do a man's torso's mysteries
Lie open to your sense of smell?

Do you—whose skin amazingly
Stretches across your swelling thighs,
Whose joints, as Solomon could see,
Are jeweled like a watch's eyes—

Imagine, with a shock, men's knees
Rock-solid like a horse's hocks,
Their shoulders with that massive ease,
Their little hips, their coarse chest-box,

Their partial intelligence,
Their danger to one's games and plans?
How can the soul have smell and sense?
Are woman's questionings like man's?

APHRODITE

Body of a girl, age undetermined,
postadolescent. Missing head, feet, hands.
Advanced state of decomposition.
Boy who found remains
did not disturb them, reports
no recent activity in area.
Officers called me into the case,
Inspector Orff, today December 4th.
Established victim carried to present location
by fall flooding of river.
Upon examination corpse showed not a sign
Of violence, except dismemberment;
About her delicate bones there climbed a vine
Of wild grape. I must report this event:
It seemed to me her bones were clothed and bright
With flesh, as they had been a year ago:
And she was beautiful. Her skin was light
As milk, but with a golden underglow:
Naked, with red–gold hair, eyes hazel–gold,
Her breasts the very rivers of desire;
Nor was it possible she could grow old:
Her knees, her lovely arms, were bathed with fire;
Her lips were open, officers, and I
Knelt down before the goddess and would die.

VII

THE KING AT SCHOOL

Ah, pulse of self, tremble of a usurping king,
Shudder so ceaseless that you'd take it for control,
Why now this quickening?
Why now this eager grieving of the soul?

Death or the threat of death would be a lightening,
A sweet reprieve, like an extra half-day off school:
This self, this makeshift thing,
Is not so hard to lose, so beautiful

You could not bear to part with it; and still the sting
Persists, so that you would turn inside out, unroll
Your moist and subtle cling
To find the sore place with its burning coal,

And let that white-hot flaw, that snake, that festering
Fall and be free, the kingdom once again be whole,
And the mad ragged king,
This gentle truant, run away from school.

WINTER STORM IN TEXAS

A delicate little thunderstorm comes about midnight;
I sit in the back veranda wearing a robe,
A haze drifts under the eave, but it's warm November;
I might as well be naked:

It is so dark not even the birds could see me,
But the black leaves of the passionflower, the tendriled
    wisteria
Shine in the distant lamplight, flash to rococo
Ornament white in the lightning.

The dripping of raindrops changes its pitch to a burble
And a heavier flaw of turbulence passes on over:
It lightens again, and the drumming slows to a patter,
A silence broken by thunder.

And this condition is almost like life itself,
When we know why we live it and know why we would
    not die;
And also like death, when we sit in its mint-smelling porch,
On the edge of the dark, an enlightenment.

FREEZE TAG

I'm It, in my big coat like a molester;
The little children cry and flee from me.
Overhead, clouds, chased by a grey northwester;
Base is a great bare-branched red oak tree.
They have commanded me to play their games,
And I, their faithful blunderbore, obey;
They dodge my clumsy hands and call me names
All afternoon of this short winter's day.
And when I've tagged a Marlyce for my larder,
Jesse, the hero, sneaks up by a tree
(When they grow up the games will all be harder)
And in an instant sets my dinner free.
The dark comes on, it's difficult to see,
One of the children has a sudden fall:
It's nothing, just a clean graze on the knee;
I hold her, a hot little animal.
And even though the evening's getting colder,
And soon we'll have to be going inside,
And they'll be very different when they're older,
And even though we're all a little tired,
And even if there never is a spring,
And even if the stars will all go cold,
The rules of the game permit no ending
And It can be a thousand years old.

FIRST SNOW

There's been the lightest sprinkling of early snow.
It lies in the palms of the leaves reflecting sky,
Delicate and girlish, lighting up the ceilings.

For days the mummied leaves have smelt of bread and
        spores;
Then gales blew down the saffron heaven-canopy.
Wet clear drops fell from the sky. This morning the light
Lifts like a stage curtain. The clocks have been put back
And it's a school holiday, and the boys sleep late;
The house smells of the first woodfire of the winter;
One of the last flies has come inside in a log.

Fall's a clearing, a paradox, a blaze of light
In the epoch of light's death. Might old age be thus?—
A lightening, a blowing down of mortality?
Every evening like a Caspar David Friedrich,
The opened sky of a starry Advent dusk, the start
Of a long Christmas holiday? And those brothers,
Playing before the woodfire in their pajamas,

What will it be for them in the breathless season
Of their father's failing strength and dawned, girlish vision,
When the old clock is put back, when the curtain rises,
When the first snow picks out the pattern of the leaves?

THE MIND'S EYE VISITS SCOTLAND

On these Hibernian scarps, winterscape by Thomson,
fletched with beeches, by Perth or Aberdeen
or Inverness, those granite-pink and smokestone towns,
purged by the empirical alkalines of Hume and Mill,
the blazing eye flies, its one nostril, its sensitive cheek
borne on a burr of wings, a cherub of Vivaldi;
released so in the body's infirmity, bound only by an old
    home's string,
pass, eye, a meter over the ground; wads of snow
bend deep the heather, yellow field grass, with underneath
the dry and twilit runways of field mice; glazed stone
where drippings flash; up the valley, where the burn
has burrowed under cowls and edged sails of snow;
no hint of the harebells underground; a street,
suddenly, with a school, apple cheeks, skaters, a dominie,
granite kirk and public house; a gouged bit of dual
    carriageway;
up onto the howling moor and down, west,
to the supernal countries of eternal spring. There they are,
as if a violet stage veil, blasted with light, were parted;
and the blue sea held them, not to fly away,
the summer islands; the flying eye grows a tear
knowing again its old gate to the summer and the west.
This eye, naked of lid or lash, the soft fool,
opens its great nostril, and its cheek feels the warm wind.
Knowing its Death here, it smells Death's salt,
the white lace mist of Death burns its membrane
as the battered wood in windows is burnt by ocean sodium.
And summer comes; the Drift's metaphysical tether
swings the heavy eye now through True Thomas' lands,
over the greenshade swales of Maeve
and back to Avalon, the apple island,
the Isle of Foals, the place of banishment,
the vale of blossom, pink panicles like butter-shells,
where the King heals him of his grievous wound.

THE ANGRY MAN

I am the jailor of a man of wrath.

I pity him, for he endures supernatural pains;
the bars bruise his forearms when he hurls at them,
transparent blood runs down his shins, and his hair
is all uncombed, his poor cheeks coarse with bristles, and
    his voice hoarse
from his commands to set him free.

It seems he would carry his wife and children to the place
he claims as his own, a clapboard shack by the sea
whose very foundation's sagged till the wooden floors,
shining with ancient polish, buckle like the scales of the sea
    monster.
But that house is condemned, although he yearns for it,

and his wife and children would die if he carried them there;
for the sight of the islands, close inshore, boiling
at reef and at prow with dangerous currents,
can sometimes become a disease of the mind,
so terribly bright is the light that pours from their barrens
    and bones.

The Government's put that part of the shore out of bounds.
The bulbous hills to the north, with their white landslips,
their snowy winds so thin they are scarcely breathable,
the islands themselves, and the gulches and slopes
that fall to the beaches, have all been laid under an
    interdiction.

If the wrathful man were to escape, he would go back
to the half-ruined house that straddles the washout

where the sandy runoff from the culvert is gullied and
    braided,
and the resin and sweetsmelling heaths and sages cling to
    their hummocks;
he'd take a great armful of cloths and rugs and again set up
    his home.

He has a darkening frown, there where he's locked in the
    library.
He'll go over to the window, and come back and tear at the
    bars.
His nearest and dearest must be protected against him.
The laws can not be permitted to be broken.
The bristly hair on his forearms and cheeks makes me pity
    him.

For sometimes the turn of his head is so gentle,
his chest heaves as if he were singing inside,
and the great overcrowded teeth in his jaws
chatter, though it is not cold. He does not resent me,
scarcely looks up when I bring him his basin of food.

It is the islands, I think, that he sings about.
Though I haven't seen them, they now come into my
    dreams,
seen from across an unkempt vegetable garden
early in spring, with tussocks of brilliant grass and daffodils
where the old stone wall slopes down into the holly-choked
    gully.

The islands are ribbed with a yellowish sandstone
that shows the terrific rise and fall of the tides.
The nearer one roars all day with the current that tows in
    the channel;
The further ones lie, still as a glass, but bluer with distance,

in seas that can turn as the day changes, to all the colors of
the rainbow.

Once, in a mirror, he caught sight of me over his shoulder.
Soon I must let the angry man go.

THE ROBBER AND THE FISHERMAN

Night after night I come to the edge of a ravaged sea
And cast my hooks and sinkers out into the stormy evening
    sky.
The green waves clap against each other, burst in white.
Soon in my great hands the rod will bend into itself
And the barb set in his exasperated jaw.

For though I've used up all my bait but two
Horned and slimy fishes that I've saved till last,
And my age has come upon me quickly, like the overcast,
I feel my strength now more than ever in its final fury.
In my dream the only question left is where to set my feet.

And he will come, the brute that followed me throughout
My child's nightmares of terror, when I could not flee
Him but by taking painfully to the air in desperate glides.
But now I seek him, and he knows it. He will come
And try to rob me of my fishes, and my hook

Will break the shelly membrane of his tongue and pierce
With a new pain his brightly painted cheek, his plates
Of scale, the bronze casque of his skull. And my line,
I've tested it and he will no more know how to escape
Than the small fly bound in the bright-eyed arachnid's web.

THE EXPEDITION

I've stayed too long upon this sunlit coast,
filling my journal with its architecture,
charming the ladies at the Governor's ball,
teaching my marksmanship to the recruits.

I've covered reams of notepaper with calculations:
imports of Belgian lace, Alsatian wine,
porcelain from China and lacquers from Japan,
the latest Mozart, Pasternak, Matisse.

Their duties do not seem outrageous;
the city even does some manufacture of its own;
you can hear excellent opera here
sung by the largely local virtuosi.

My visits to the inland haciendas
have instructed me upon the politics of manners;
the fathers are Homeric, leonine;
the sons are cultured and the daughters captivating.

But I have put it off for far too long.
The time has come to strike for the interior.
This strangest of expeditions will need preparation;
already it is weeks since the last full rains.

There'll be no bearers on this journey.
I'll leave all instruments behind.
No tents, no axes, and no cameras,
no radio, no carrier pigeons.

For this exploit I must go unaccommodated.
Of course I'll leave my evening clothes behind,
my black silk hat, my diamond pin, my tails,
even the crimson ribbon of my order.

My honors must be those that show upon my body.
For this time there's no camouflage will serve.
My khaki shirts, my rifle, my Havanas
must all be left behind to await return.

This journey to the forest must be naked.
Those colors I must know touch through the skin;
The people I shall meet won't recognize me
Unless I'm stripped like Jesus when he died.

And I'm not even sure they'll recognize me
being, after all these years, hardly their own.
But, more dismaying, will I know them then
when they come from the trees, feathered and bound with
    gold?

Among those waterfalls, those screaming apes,
those ghostly cockatoos so beautiful,
those orchises, those giant waterlilies,
shall I go mad and miss the moment of discovery?

I must go naked, that my feet
may be inoculated by the poison thorns,
that in the jungle pools I be not cumbered,
that all the tongues of Europe should fall from my tongue.

Perhaps I am too old for this adventure,
being, as who reminds me not, something distingué.
but the old thews throb as if I'd taken
this journey as a boy first turning into man.

And if I go there pure, no diamond
hidden between the labia and gum,
no book nor tape recorder taped to breast or thigh,
the monster-doors will open, and I'll be let in.

For those appalling fires are my own,
those snakes and scorpions my ancestors,
those witches that shake bitter medicine on me
are my old servants, from before the university.

And when I pass the ordeal of the leopard
and when the jaguar has let me go by,
and when the golden lion has obeyed me,
I'll come to where she waits for me, and know

In her fierce eyes the passion that I lost,
the secret of my many cowardices,
the bitter reason for my spites, my littleness,
my lethargy, and my paralysis,

and by her side I'll see the other one,
the hero with his arms folded in gold,
the one I left behind, my enemy,
and look upon his face, and know my own.

ENGLISH RENAISSANCE PORTRAITS

The faces of my English ancestors
Like speaking pictures, ask me with their eyes
What I have made, what acted for what cause,
What claim, renunciation, sacrifice.

Their eyes, as dark as melancholy, burn
With an ardor that one day sacked Cadiz,
In faces nobly pale, perceptive, stern,
With beard well cut, as a good courtier's is.

Essex and Raleigh, Percy, Drake, and Donne,
Howard and Grenville, and the prince of peers,
Sidney, who dined in Aedes Christi, as I've done—
All of those dead and reckless chevaliers.

These times do not afford a test of spurs:
Still I have kept myself in readiness
To do what body may when spirit stirs.
To watch and wait's a kind of knightliness.

The realm they founded in Virginia
They named Atlantis, Eden, Fairyland;
I call upon my country sadlier:
Ah, my America, my newfound land.

Those faces are my own and their proud verse
Sings like the fatal engine of my genes.
I stand here for your play. If the time's worse,
The glory's greater when I speak your scenes.

The Ghost in the Airplane

Again I'm flying from my life, my life.
Each time I come it is a bleeding
A little from the sacrificial knife,
Enough for a signature or a seeding.

And each time I am passed along the duct
Into a bright or darkling city,
My past self is a ghost that is sucked
In, out, like the unquenching sigh of pity.

You, Fred, what are you but a wisp of gas
Writ with a hundred words of knowing?—
That will be rushed beyond the white dunes as
The sea mist when the morning wind is blowing;

Or shall some subtle flaw, or terrorist,
Pluck this stressed shred of aluminum,
And I with brief thanks cease then to exist,
Giving my seed and blood to the continuum?

KERN COUNTY REGIONAL AIRPORT

Some day, having quite forgotten who I am,
having left my baggage, my contact lenses in the airplane,
during this slightly-longer-than-usual stopover
I shall walk out into the mild California air
and disappear from everything I have been.

It was not a bad life, that one which I led:
a life of amazing effort, of agonizing patience,
but very full of things considered good,
much love, of a kind, mostly unconnected,
a life of vanity and of purposeless striving.

And what would I do in Kern County with my
two hundred dollars in twenties, my myopic eyes,
the clothes I stand up in, my good will and strong body,
my sleepiness in the afternoon, some shreds of reading,
the story of my life like a half-understood dream?

VIII

MIRANDA

(in the house of a suicide)

Prospero dowered his daughter here with this island:
where everything, million-pinned redwood, hummingbird,
malachite holly leaf, sweet honeysuckle,
elbowed and feathery ridges, thistledown
going wherever it wants to go, fog in the vales,
everything presses itself on the sight like a dream,
manifold, bright, just as the vision expected.
The hills of wild rye rise up, like cumulus, golden
over your brow, and below, like a chasm, the long
larch spears reach up to your feet.
But on this island Prospero's daughter died;
by her own hand she canceled these horizons.
Ask her whatever question you will, she burns
out of the blue sky, terrible, mute.

FOR ROBERTA

Two ghosts contest this body deep with pain:
Death, large and easy, like a gentleman
With a cigar, who can well take his time,
And some bright essence, like a tremulous flame.

Ah, now she is already halfway in
To that dark empery of Proserpine,
Her pomegranate seeds like rubies glow,
Those brilliant tumors, but the embryo

Of a new life of which she is the vial,
Whose cheeks blaze with miraculous denial,
Whose laughter and whose fear take the heart
Of the cruel poet, a Pluto in his art;

O she will make the shades in Hades dance
With her bright cheek, her intelligent glance;
If her disease were catching, which it is,
Still it were worth the risking of a kiss;

Roberta vanishing, Roberta rosy,
Crimson and eveblue flowers in a posy,
O nosegay who makes light of all the grief,
Be the stern cicerone of my belief;

And both your spirits, cancer and the scream
Of the freed spirit singing in the flame,
Grasp the full shuttle of my artery,
Sibyl, the heartbeat of the poetry.

THE DISTRIBUTION
—in Memory of Victor Turner

Now he's all given away,
all the soft parts:
his tongue, his ruptured gullet, and his eyes
(which once were bright brown darts),
his poor shins, pink and grey
with their hereditary skin disease;
all that wonderful talk;
his busted liver and eroded hips
which made a struggle of his gallant walk,
made permanent his old Gaswegian pub-raconteur's stance
(but still, he'd always dance);
his Santa Claus's nose, sardonic lips,
his little hands with their gamekeeper's thumb,
his dentures, which he frightened children by,
all given away;
the foxy eyebrows, now quite still and dumb,
his brain where all the human dialects,
the world's temples, here only not at war,
made solemn sex;
his shoes, his three old pairs of pants,
frayed terribly for such a famous man's;
the memories of dawn in Africa;
it is as if he wore
a white garment, and they took
the parts from him he innocently gave
forgetting the blood that shook
upon it from his cruelly ransacked nave;
all of it given away, every last part:
the puns, the snorting smile; he would save
nothing back, all he had he gave,
and last of all, his heart.

FOR JOHN AND NANCY VAN NESS
—in Memory of Julie

As kind hosts show their treasure
To the admiring guest,
They, quiet in their pleasure,
Indulged our interest:

A girl as clear and single
As is the lily flower—
Where wit and sweetness mingle,
The soul puts forth its power;

And when I learnt the shadow
That clung to her bright life,
And knew of the bravado
She showed before its knife,

I was abashed, a tyro
Bowed by a work of art,
Would leave until tomorrow
The reckoning of my heart,

And never thanked them truly
For what they let me see—
How richly and how cruelly
Love twists its last degree.

ON THE PAINS OF TRANSLATING MIKLÓS RADNÓTI

(The great Hungarian poet shot by the Nazis in 1944. His mother and twin brother died in childbirth.)

And now I too must wrestle with a brother
Whose dead limbs cumber me within the womb,
Whose grief I pity, but whose cord of nurture
Glides dreadful and unseen in this blind gloom.

That angel, who is Michael in my language,
Knew how to die, knew how to share a grave;
Sometimes he almost overcrows my spirit,
His great feathered wings beating in the cave—

My elder brother died as I first opened
My lips in speech instead of in a scream;
Now he returns to claim the voice I borrowed,
Now he returns, the hero of my dream.

How can I share the lifeblood of our mother?
How can I let his dead voice steal my breath?
But how indeed could I deny my brother
Who, reckless, bought my birthright with his death?

For all alone among that generation
He kept the faith that I have made my name,
That ancient grace, that hard emancipation,
The love of form that touches us like flame.

What can I do but open to his service ·
The pulse and wordstream of the mother tongue?
Thus I subdue myself and hear him singing
Out of the land of shades where none have sung.

Could I, the Western democrat, professor,
Father, essayist, of middle age,
Be given any greater gift than this is,
To share the passion of his vassalage?

IX

On Sitting Down with Zsuzsanna Ozsvath to Translate Radnóti

All mortal courses bleed and burn with trouble,
I must do evil wheresoever I turn,
We wander, brutal, scared, among the rubble,
Loss and despair the only way we learn.
Savage and narrow ideologies consume us,
Beauty is torn among the wavering crowd,
Darkness of mind and grief and hate entomb us
And the child's soiled innocence wails aloud.
All I can do entangles me still further
Within the ill-doing of the thirsty past;
I mar the creature I would mold and mother
And rage at the ill-shaped turns my love to dust.

Now I wash off the blood, and feel the calm:
This hour I shall do good, and do no harm.

INCARNATENESS

My karma clots on me like human blood,
Whose fibers are the trains of consequence
That bind the mortal world of bad and good,
Linking desire with act, and truth with sense.

Armored, insensate, like a plated knight,
I carry, belted, rage and love and greed,
Am a householder and defend the right;
My sons—my love aches for them—bear my seed.

Here between death and death I smile to find
Myself a great man of affairs:
With friends, with allies, passions of the mind,
My books, my gardens, duties, habits, cares.

Sometimes my gopis, spirit-sisters, seem
To offer me simplicity's delight;
But I am bound to this laborious dream,
May not yet open to the unveiled light.

There at the center of illusion stands
A woman, beautiful, a bended bow
Of fate, tension, duty. And in her hands
My poetries all break, all pride's brought low,

No custom lasts into unconsciousness,
No spiritual closure will suffice,
No wisdom can aspire to perfectness,
No kiss be ever undertaken twice.

Lady, you are the hardness of the real:
My center and dismissal from the wheel.

RETURN

Again and after all, my subtle wife,
I wake up in your arms like a new man,
Having through labyrinths and poisoned trenches,
Shot at and hunted, found the one way back
Into the inner landscape of my life.

Ah, it was terrible. At first the sky was blue,
And the earth smiled, the fig tree put out fruit,
The people welcomed me, they carried palms,
They heard my words and thought them beautiful,
Until they learned what I would have them do.

I was the stranger then, the ghost-face man,
The bad dog driven out with all the sins:
And worse, they sent as if to be a comfort
Demons in female dress who tempted me
To give myself unto a courtesan;

But though I wept and wrung my arms in pain,
Fought on bad ground, lost two fights out of three,
Was made a spectacle for others' uses,
And never represented as I am,
Unpitying myself I've come again

Into the sacred threshold of your sky,
Uncaught, unbroken, though a little weary,
And sick with all the evil I have seen;
I offer you my honor still untarnished,
My will engaged yet till the day I die:

And step into the stillness of the moon
And the seven stars that shine upon your ground,
Where the blue silk of your pavilion
Makes ruffles in the apple-scented wind
That blows between the midnight and the noon.

THE INDWELLING

For twelve years I endured the cares of the world,
Thinking my time of paradise was gone forever;
But paradise had never passed away
Through all that vain endeavor.

And it is in me still, this gold calm of the mustardseed,
This gold spindle wound with the golden thread,
Whose points are mounted in the socket-bone
Of the heart and of the head.

It is my angel that mounts me, that hums in me, that never
        leaves me:
For whom my self is but the veil of burial, the shroud,
The caul of thin saliva on the tongue
That lets it speak aloud.

And who is the angel? O he is a mild cantata out of cream,
Ruler of a certain fertile principality in heaven,
And it is strange, that his time shall not come
For seven ages times seven.

And in this house that leaks from seven days of rain,
Where the body, and its brief self, sit writing by the
        gramophone,
And the cold drops roll on the yellow leaves
And branch the windowpane,

The angel makes his throne.

PICTURE POSTCARDS:
A TRAVEL DIARY FOR AUGUST 1989

I.
On the London-to-Paris Train

I'm carried swiftly through the fields of England;
Soon I'll be rushing through the fields of France.
And again the call comes to attempt the passage
Of the soul, to take its sullen chance.

Il faut laisser maison, vergers, jardins:
Radnóti quoted Ronsard so, which I
Translated with a quiver of the heart
And now remember with a restless sigh.

What would it have me do?—the train
Casts shadows on the wet and glittering plains
Of dawn, and rushes through the trees—
What sickness of the spirit gives such pains,

Such shortness of the breath, such cramps, such joy,
Permits no diagnosis, defies cure,
Beckons me to such oceans of such loss,
And will not suffer wisdom to endure?

II.
Bavaria: Morning, Going East

This time it's the green fields of Germany:
Mountain-horizons, just as I recall;
Already onion-cupolas foreshadow
The greater Orient, its golden pall.

Nach östen, then, I am compelled to follow
In the blurred footsteps of a children's crusade;
But still the green grail flees away before me,
My questions cannot pierce the masquerade.

The welling rivers of the land of France,
Their deep weirs and their poplar groves, were still
The borrowings of others' acts of vision,
However bright the poppies on the hill;

In Paris with my friend the analyst,
The answers told me only what I knew;
Last night I woke just as we crossed the border,
And in the dark the subtle sickness grew.

III.
Beside the Danube, a Day Later

Such armies dragged their way across this land!
In blue shakos, and scarlet frogged with brass,
Their squares and regiments would undulate
Over the hills and vales like stands of grass;

And then the smoke would billow, and the corn
Would be laid flat as by a windblown rain;
And then those armies passed away, and others
Grew up, and fought, and fell, and so again.

We're flying by the river, where the trees
Sometimes close in to hide its silver glow,
Sometimes stand back to show a sullen light
That gleams in battered plates from swell and flow.

Was it my death that I have gone to find?
My age has come upon me; I prefer

The silence of first class over the sweat
And cheerful rucksacks of the corridor;

Yesterday, in Munich, with an old friend,
We did not listen to each other's news;
He worried for his mother; I was tired;
We saw upon each other time's grey bruise.

The thought of rivers, time, and fought-out wars,
My fading strength, the loneliness of rain,
And knowing all that I have done before,
Is all too much for me to start again.

But still there's something more that calls me on.
There is another battle yet to fight,
A river of the soul that I must follow
Down to an ocean of unhidden light.

IV.

A Street Café at Night; Indoors, a Wedding Reception

And now in Budapest, this sweet old city,
The town of humankind where the great stream
Pours through the bridges, lit with lamps and signs,
I take up once again my unscanned dream.

The peaches and the plums of Budapest!
What an ingratitude, where the gold East
Turns like a sunflower through freckled August,
To turn away in sorrow from the feast!

Festival city, whose unburied dead
Are now laid peaceful under fruited trees,
Whose moment comes to step upon the stage
And sing the ancient newborn mysteries,

Forgive me if, a shadow at the door,
While the veiled bride dances with her groom,
And the great chestnuts fan their vaulted leaves,
And children stay up late, and roses bloom,

Forgive me if I waste this last of summer
Upon a quest that, if it should succeed,
Would only turn the golden light of knowledge
Upon a thing better perhaps left hid:

My own soul, which is still and all unburied,
Because one cannot kill what has no being:
The self that is an emptiness that sees,
That is not seen, but is the space of seeing;

Yet, like all dead things, makes a hole in God,
Insults the nuptials of the living world,
Groans like a torment, like a cracked machine,
And craves the darkness where its bones are hurled;

That twisted omega whose truth is zero,
That contravortex of contorted time,
That light which turns to darkness when it turns
Upon itself, the turner of the rhyme;

And this disgusting thing, this piss-soaked rag,
This old, exhausted consciousness, must seek
Redemption in the knowledge of itself,
Holding its nose against its own rank reek;

Neglecting, in the glory of the summer,
The golden city in its soft rebirth,
The loveliness of man and child and woman,
The bounty and the fruit time of the earth.

V.

Budapest: Morning, Two Days Later

(In the background of this poem were the recent reburial of Imre Nagy, the murdered leader of the 1953 Hungarian Revolution against the Soviet Union, the recent burial of János Kádár, the communist puppet who replaced him, and the presumed exhumation of Sándor Petöfi, the heroic nineteenth-century poet who fought with the Hungarian rebels against the Austrian Empire.)

There's no escape from history. The city
Bellows with tourists, bursts with refugees;
The beaten fabric frays and shows its bones,
And the brown leaves are falling from the trees.

There is no place, among the pipes and sewers,
The cables and the subways of the living,
To give the crowded dead their burial,
And so they walk the streets all unforgiving.

My body is becoming such a city:
Fragile and shaking with the weight of years,
A motor whose alignments have decayed,
That overheats and strips its belts and gears.

This night I dreamed they had replaced my brain:
I saw the old one, cleaned and neatly scraped,
Laid on a slab with others to be sold,
And wondered if the memories were kept.

I woke in darkness; and my life has failed,
My work has not been worth the love I'm given;
There are no new brains to replace the old,
No sacrifice whereby the soul is shriven.

I woke in darkness. Now the light has come,
A sweet blue haze upon the roofs and trees.
Illusion, river mist, or traffic fumes:
Dawn charms and softens night's realities.

VI.

In Graz, Austria, for a Conference

It's raining wildly in the town of Graz.
The onion-dome nearby is wet with rain.
The river Mur makes heaps against its pilings.
I have retreated westwards from the pain.

This place so orderly (rain in the park),
The trains on time (rain in the railway yard),
The hotel comfortable (but the rain),
All these conspire to soften what's so hard,

To quilt and color with their flattery
The fiction of the honored public man,
Poet and scholar and authority:
But still the darkened violence of the rain

Threatens all dwelling, and could yet uproot
The stone foundations of this quiet hotel,
The fragrant trees planted along the park,
The clock tower with its sweet and punctual bell.

VII.

10 A.M. in Europe; 3 A.M. in Texas

Mei Lin sleeps on the far side of the world.
That lucid consciousness of hers, severe,
Honest beyond compassion, beyond hope,
Is for this time uncoupled from its sphere;

And now perhaps that other side of her,
That strange dark garden, very sharp and far,
Its airy rocks laid out with Chinese charm,
Is open to the bright light of its star;

And the quiet spirit of the gardener
Has taken leave of gardening for an hour,
And come to keep me company as I
Sit by this rainslick Austrian clock tower;

And like the Austrian Maria-Hilfer
She mitigates the emptiness and fear,
And brings a teacup full of Chinese dreams
To help me carry what I cannot bear.

VIII.

Going Further East

I dream of traveling by train across
The hills and plains of Macedonia.
It is the same dream I have often dreamed,
Lit by the same anxious euphoria.

I wake, and it is just as in the dream.
The two worlds meet, and merge; reality
Is backlit to its depths by the dream light;
There is no gap between to see and be.

And what's it like, this land of waking dream?
You hear a cock crow through the beveled glass,
And see a shepherdess in a red dress
Leading her sheep across the flowering grass.

IX.

Ochrid, Six Days before Return

And now I've come to where the river Dream
Enters and leaves a lake that's bottomless,
Whose shining water stretches to a mist
Horizonless, shadowless, limitless.

It is the same depth that the sightless eyes
Of ikons in the sanctuary wall
Stare into through the war-burned centuries:
The same last answer to the aching call.

The self is but a skin of pigment laid
Upon the surface of the divine dream;
This dance of Macedonia, the friends, the wine,
The roasted fishes in the walnut cream,

The Adriatic profiles of the girls,
The halting flow of words and poetry,
This very pen-twitch now of consciousness,
Are but the ripples of an endless sea.

X.

The Token Taken Back

But how may one who in his undeserving
Is given such a vision of the soul,
Whose self, that wretched thing, has fallen silent
Enough to hear the breathing of the whole,

How can he now return into the world,
Shoulder once more the worn yoke of desire,
And play the actor on the thumping stage
Who has walked calm and silent in the fire?

How can I paint a mask upon my face,
And measure fellow creatures with a grade,
How can I shake the thundersheet of power,
How fill in all the moments I am paid?

Time is such labor, death so far away
(That moment when the waters are all still,
The curtains drawn, the breath all satisfied),
How can I climb the last steps of the hill?

And all this is a kind of laziness.
The Turkish peasants, in the weary sun
Winnowing grain, are all as wise as I:
I too must finish what I have begun.

What of the soul then, that I must forget,
That shining moiety of the great light,
That still, unmanning glory I must shun,
That depth with its betrayals of delight?

Let it go join the ikons on the wall,
Let this gold moment lose itself within
The blue glimmer of the lake's great eye,
And so I will continue in the sin

Of life, until the moment that I die.
But will there be no keepsake of the time
When all was equal in the blazing sky
Of lake and heaven, like a perfect rhyme?

Will I take nothing back into the world?
This morning in the marketplace I bought
A silver pendant, like a black mandala.
It's very old, and curiously wrought.

Within its outer rings of ornament,
That stand for the world's blessings and its harms,
Enthroned is a madonna all of fire
Where a firechild sits in her fiery arms.

There's almost no time to complete the poem,
Yet I must finish this that I've begun;
The silver image of the spirit's home,
This token, I take back to give my son.

XI.

Skopje: Toward Evening

The summer's spent. In the slant rain of autumn
I walk beside the Vardar, in the smell
Of fallen plane leaves sour and melancholy:
My soaked shoes make me shiver with the chill.

And night falls on this Oriental city;
The mosques are darkened with the fitful rain;
The people are indoors in their apartments,
Perhaps I'll never come this way again.

I meet a poet in a small café;
We drink a shot of slivovitz together
And dine on sausage behind misted glass
And go out afterwards into the weather

And see, among the blackness of the clouds,
A few stars like the speckles of an opal,
Or, in the words of an old Turkish song,
The little windows of Constantinople.

XII.

Gipsy Summer: For Naum Panofski

And now it's time to go. The sky has cleared;
The gorges of the Vardar, and the ranges,
Are bright and cold as we drive south to Greece:
Death is the big name for the little changes.

In Thessaloniki a cutting wind
Blows by the promenade and stills the sea;
The awnings flap, the tables are deserted,
And time has come and put its hand on me.

But there is yet to come the gipsy summer,
For the old folk, another month of toil:
The sunflowers, that droop their heavy heads,
Must all be cut and crushed down for their oil.

Envoi: On the Plane

It all reels backward, like a spinning tape:
The Black Gate, and the hills of yesterday,
The vales of Serbia, the river Danube,
The fields of Germany, all whirl away;

The English coast, the woods and little towns,
The old Atlantic blown to a dark blue;
My soul's axle, my only native country,
Mei Lin, I'm coming home to you.

First Base

I.

This ancient thing that must be done
Requires the death of one man's time,
A prayer before it is begun,
The island quiet of rhyme.

Just as twelve years ago we fell
To madness that begot a son
And broke all caution in the spell
Of conjugation,

So now the fire must be set,
The dishes put away, the door
Locked fast that nothing hoarse might fret
The birth of metaphor.

Am I a fool to solemnize
With invocations to the muses
These mere suburban alibis,
Confessions, or excuses?

Come, lady, then, and lead the fool
Across the freeway by the mall,
And past the public swimming-pool
Left of the city hall,

And out through naked tracts and parks,
To where the sunlit streets are bare,
To outfields where the meadowlarks
Tweedle upon the air.

II.

Honor forbids my son to notice me,
Setting his baseball cap against the glare.
First baseman, he must watch the catcher's sign,
Intimidate the batter with his stare,
Anchor the fielding into one design,
And be the very animal and form
Of his position in the baseball team,
As bulls and meadowlarks fulfill the norm
Designate for them by the chromosome.
These cardinals, these cubs, these senators,
How perfectly professional they seem,
Eleven-year-old gum-chewing matadors!
Wordsworth thought such a theater would come
Between the boy and his eternal home,
But what if we must all invent our being?
Is then the "master-light of all our seeing"
The actor's concentration on his part?
Then why this pain that brushes at my heart?

III.

I am a stranger from another universe;
This is as strange to me as the horse games of Turkestan—
Carcass of lamb that is torn among bridegiving tribesmen.
I am from Marx's Europe, the England of slums and the
        Beatles,
I am from Arthur's table, from the France of Cézanne and
        Courbet,
I am the last colonial, the sun went down on my childhood
In Northern Rhodesia, the drums rumbled all night and
My father read to me Shakespeare in the roar of the pressure
        lamp;
I am from Virgil's Campania, from Homer's Peloponnese;

My mind was formed by the Huxleys, by Einstein and
    Wittgenstein,
Eliot, Yeats, and the songs of the English Renaissance;
I am the heir of Hegel, of Nietzsche, of Freud,
Born and raised in the throb of the flying bomb.
My weather's the fitful rain of Europe,
The smoky taste of the last of the Industrial Revolution,
The ambiguous cloudlands and definite soil of the Old
    World,
The damp snow on the bus-stop bench that seeped through
    my
Trouser pocket and soaked my packet of Woodbines,
My wadded handkerchief, my pink ten-shilling note.

And what am I doing in Plano, Texas, on this hot after-
Noon in summer, the thunderclouds clear on the horizon
    like
Grotesque pieces of matte sunlit china, like
Stuffed toys to be given to baby dinosaurs, like the
Sound of a big rock band tuning up in a stadium?
What am I doing in Plano, with its malls and pyramids?

IV.

But what have they been doing there in Europe?
My brave son Ben, watching the pitch come down,
Must teach impossible progenitors
How to be parents to a Texan child;
And over there in Warsaw, Budapest,
And East Berlin they wash the bloody hands
Of Beethoven and Sartre, and gently show
Their blood-drunk parents just how to be free.
All that I know of baseball comes from Ben.
How is it I am rooted now in him?
Where did he get that authenticity
That makes him pluck with fine unconsciousness

The wrinkle from his pants, and crack his gum?
Raised in a laundry in the Pennine Hills,
His mother is Chinese and loves Racine.

At school they teach him (in the best modern way)
How Hannibal's elephants crossed the Alps,
How to bow smoothly between bridge and thumb,
Of the white ratios of geometry:
But what is it makes him a Texican?

V.

The new world being born, I helped it come.
Out of its mother's belly,
of all its ancestors
the fruit, of many seeds, mine being one,
it turned its head and smiled.
Do I betray it now, with this private consciousness,
this slacker form, designed
to opt out of the game?—
thus wars and holocausts too cruel to name—?
I fall into the rhyme,
betray the betrayal.

Evening's coming. Under the stormcloud
the tired sunlight on the bleachers turns to orange
the white logos on the parents' T-shirts,
the white parabolas of their Nike Airs.

VI.

Now already the knotted concepts I shaped to stagger
The cruel march of historicism, the smooth slide I polished
At the edge between word and world to trap the haters of
    humankind,

My carillons of mental bells poured in their melodious
    foundries,
All these are owned by younger men and women, scholars,
Poets, and they know them and use them better than I ever
    could,
Being accustomed, as I was not, to my newfangled
    landscape.
The birds and animals are no longer shy around my
    constructions.
Their masters, the shepherds and shepherdesses, sing them
    my songs.
Happy, I pass my possessions on to them; now I prepare for
    my
Metamorphosis into another being, smelling of
Evening, of thunderstorms over the horizon, of darkening
    grass.

VII.

But soon the floodlights are turned on,
As Plano tilts against the sky,
And endless time piles up above
The ballfield's little lighted octagon;

An orange skin of evening glows
Beneath the bluelit towers of cloud;
A few drops fall, the game goes on;
The warm, coyote-smelling wind still blows;

The crackle of an utterance
Above the curvature of plain
Echoes in rumbles from the ground
And holds the players in a moment's trance;

The batter hits a loaded fly,
Ben edges under it, elbows

His baseball cap out of his eye,
And takes it quickly, fires it home, as I

Marvel how second nature grows
Its subtle graft upon the first;
And now another lightning burst
Has turned the clouds into a purple rose.